From Here to There

A Traveler's Guide to Cultural Experiences

Table of Contents

Chapter 1. Introduction

Embark on an exhilarating journey with every turn of the page in our latest Special Report, "From Here to There: A Traveler's Guide to Cultural Experiences." This lively compilation transcends the common definition of travel, connecting curious souls with the profound depth of diverse cultures the world over. Travel is not merely about jetting off to breathtaking destinations, but a stimulating voyage of understanding customs, food, music, and stories that have shaped societies for generations. Every page of this report is brimming with vibrant photographs, heartwarming anecdotes, helpful tips, and expertly-curated itineraries that will ignite your wanderlust. Come, let's traverse this globe together and unfold the unexplored tapestry of cultural experiences – because we believe every journey begins with a single page!

Chapter 2. Globetrotting Basics: How to Plan for Cultural Immersion

Travel planning, at its core, isn't merely about booking flights, hotels, and noting down places to visit. It is about immersing oneself fully in the sights, sounds, tastes, and stories embedded in the heart of every locale. Encountering cultures directly, understanding their histories, customs, cuisine, music, and the lives of the people will transform your perspective on travel.

2.1. Understanding Cultural Immersion

Cultural immersion is about integrating oneself with a new or alien culture. It's not about spending a week at a luxury resort but about experiencing life as locals do. Whether it's partaking in their traditional ceremonies, eating street food, understanding their history, or learning a few words in their language, it's about stepping out of your comfort zone and seeing the world through their eyes.When you immerse yourself in a different culture, you are opening your horizons to a whole new world and understanding humanities better.

2.2. The Value of Cultural Awareness and Sensitivity

Cultural immersion commences with awareness and sensitivity towards the culture we aim to explore. Acquiring an understanding of do's and don'ts, learning a few words of the native language, or understanding the traditions can make a huge difference in your

Chapter 4. Food for the Soul: The Global Gastronomy Journey

Fuel is not just a necessity for our bodies, but for our souls. With every morsel we ingest, we partake in a vital, shared ritual and savor the essence of cultures built over millennia. So fasten your seatbelts as we take you on a mouthwatering journey across the globe, sampling some of the world's most delectably irresistible fare.

4.1. Forks in the Road: Understanding Global Eating Manners

Before we delve into the heart of global gastronomy, it's important to understand that how we eat is as significant as what we eat. Each nation has unique dining manners, and respecting these traditions is a significant part of the cultural experience.

In Japan, for example, it's customary to say 'itadakimasu' (I gratefully receive) before a meal, and 'gochisosama' (thanks for the meal) after finishing. The chopsticks should never be stuck upright in your rice, as it's reminiscent of offerings at a funeral. In certain parts of India, eating with your hands is more than just a practicality; it's a way to connect with the food and infuse it with one's personal energy.

In sharp contrast, Ethiopian etiquette dictates using only the right hand for eating, typically using injera - a unique, spongy bread - to scoop up various dishes. Etiquette varies extensively, and while it may seem intricate and even overwhelming, a little attention and curiosity can go a considerable way in embracing local customs and building connections.

4.2. The Mediterranean Odyssey: A Symphony of Flavors

The Mediterranean diet, declared a UNESCO Intangible Cultural Heritage, invites you into the warm embrace of sun, sea, and sublime flavors. Owing to the region's rich biodiversity and cultural tapestry, Mediterranean food offers an eclectic spread of dishes.

From Greece's minced-meat-filled gemista, to Spain's hearty paella, and Italy's globally beloved pizza and pasta, each dish tells a unique story of its place of origin. Not to mention the omnipresent and versatile olive oil, a hallmark of Mediterranean cuisine, running like a golden thread through its culinary framework.

Try your hand at home with a simple Greek salad or Italian Caprese - fresh tomatoes, cucumbers, feta or mozzarella cheeses, olives and a generous drizzle of olive oil. Paired with freshly baked bread, you have a simple yet delectably satisfying Mediterranean meal.

4.3. A Taste of the Orient: Exploring East Asia's Culinary Richness

Traveling eastward, we arrive in Asia, a continent known for its breathtaking diversity in food. Here, street stalls are treasure troves of taste and local flair.

Japan's sushi and ramen, South Korea's spicy kimchi and bibimbap, China's dim sum and Peking duck, or Vietnam's fragrant pho - each dish not only bursts with umami but also offers insight into the history and ethos of its native country. Spices, seafood, rice, and broth form the base of many Asian dishes, creating complex layers of flavors and textures that characterize this culinary tradition.

Delve into these cultures through their staples. Cook a simple bowl of ramen at home with instant noodles, chicken stock, fresh veggies, and a boiled egg. Season with soy sauce, or if daring, a dash of kimchi for an extra kick.

4.4. Soul Food of the Americas: A Forkful of Heritage

Signifying a canvas as diverse as its landscape, American cuisine brims with savory, sweet, spicy, and everything in-between. From Southern comfort food of fried chicken, cornbread and collard greens, to Mexican tacos al pastor, Argentine asado, or the oh-so Canadian poutine – the Americas offer culinary adventures studded with robust flavors, colorful ingredients, and multicultural infusions.

Whether it's the USA's apple pie oozing homely warmth, or the fruity tanginess of a Peruvian ceviche, each nation, and indeed each region within these nations, offers a unique bite of its heritage.

Try one of the more accessible American comfort foods: grilled cheese. A griddle-toasted sandwich loaded with melting cheese, it's best enjoyed with a bowl of tomato soup. This simplistic yet fulfilling meal is a classic staple across American households.

4.5. Conclusion: A Moveable Feast

Our global gastronomy trip is, in effect, a testament to the infinite variety that pervades the human existence - the tastes, traditions, and tales woven around food that keep the world colorful and connected.

At its core, food bridges gaps, forges friendships, and fuels appreciation for other cultures. So prepare your apron, sharpen your culinary skills, and open your mind to the deliciously diverse world of global gastronomy. Each dish you try or cook, each etiquette you learn is a passport stamp in your gastronomical journey.

Remember, in the symphony of world cuisines, there's always a new note to discover and savor. Don't just eat to live; live to eat, and eat to explore! Let this guide serve as a roadmap, allowing you to traverse through historical fermentations, regional specialities, and world's kitchens. This is not the final destination but only the beginning of a lifelong journey for your taste buds, satiating your wanderlust one bite at a time.

Chapter 5. Voices of the World: A Dive into Languages and Accents

The symphony of languages and accents across the globe bears the mark of our diverse cultures and histories. Every word uttered, however mundane, is an echo of our ancestors, the remnant of some ancient tale, and a testament to our rich and varied lifestyles. Meet the world through its voices!

5.1. The Linguistic Landscape

The world is home to over 7,000 active languages. This linguistic diversity is a testament to human adaptability and innovation. The largest of these languages by number of speakers are Mandarin Chinese, Spanish, English, and Hindi, but size isn't the only measure of a language's importance. Thousands of smaller languages, each with their unique charm and character, add to the global linguistic mosaic.

Around 4,000 of the world's languages have fewer than 10,000 speakers, and these tend to be clustered in regions of high biodiversity, suggesting a link between linguistic and biological diversity. Papua New Guinea, for instance, has over 800 languages, making it the most linguistically diverse place on the planet.

On the other side of the spectrum, the 'global languages' like English, Spanish, and French, are widely spoken and have spread well beyond their original borders thanks to historical, political, and economic reasons. These languages connect people across continents, fostering international communication and cooperation.

Just as languages vary, so do the scripts in which they are written.

The world's writing systems are innumerable, ranging from the alphabet-based scripts of Latin, Greek, and Cyrillic to the syllabaries of Japanese Kana, and the logograms of Chinese Hanzi.

5.2. Exploring Accents

An accent is how a language is spoken by a particular group of people. It may reflect their geographic location, social class, or ethnic community. No two accents are the same, and individuals often have their unique speech patterns - a testament to the dynamism of language.

In England alone, for example, you could encounter the broad Yorkshire accents, the crisp Received Pronunciation (often associated with the British upper class and BBC broadcasts), the lilting Welsh accents, and many more. All of a nation's accents grouped together form its 'dialect continuum', a spectrum of speech variety often influenced by geography.

In the United States, accents can vary wildly from the nasal twangs of the Deep South to the rhotic pronunciations of the Boston area. Similarly, the Spanish language, while maintaining some universal characteristics across its speakers, has distinct accents in every nation - from the lisping Castilian Spanish, to the rapid-fire Caribbean Spanish, and the seseo of Latin American Spanish.

Accents contribute to personal and communal identities, acting as social markers and adding to communication's color and diversity. This, ultimately, is what makes the planet's symphony of voices so rich and intriguing.

5.3. Language Death and Revitalization

Sadly, many languages aren't merely small; they're dying. Globalization and modernization often lead to 'language shift' where communities abandon their native tongue for a more dominant or prestigious language. This process, when complete, leads to 'language death.'

It is estimated that one language is disappearing every two weeks. These losses impact not just on our linguistic diversity, but on our cultural diversity. Each language, dialect or accent represents a unique way of seeing the world and is often woven with local wisdom, folklore, and knowledge systems. When a language dies, a unique worldview dies with it.

However, there's a silver lining. Efforts worldwide aim at language revitalization, that is, bringing dying or dead languages back to life. Such initiatives often come from the communities themselves and range from implementing immersion education (like in the case of the Maori in New Zealand) to digitizing language resources for easy and universal access.

5.4. The Power of your Voice

Languages and accents are an essential part of our identities, connecting us to our families, communities, and histories. Recognizing and celebrating linguistic diversity leads to more inclusive societies where people feel valued for their unique voices.

On this note, the next time you pick up your travel book or plan your itinerary, don't forget to include language immersion - take a local language class, try a new script, or attune your ears to the unique accents you encounter. The voices of the world are waiting to share their stories with you; all you need to do is listen.

Chapter 6. Traditions and Celebrations: A Universal Calendar of Festivities

The world thrums to a collective rhythm as it dances to the harmony of varied traditions and celebrations.

6.1. New Year Celebrations

Where else to begin but at the inception of a new year, a symbolic new beginning that is celebrated across the globe! From the thunderous fireworks of Sydney, Australia's Sydney Harbour to the sobriety of Japan's Omisoka, each region welcomes the new year in its unique style. The Chinese Lunar New Year, also known as Spring Festival, engulfs China and many parts of the world in a festive frenzy with its red lanterns, lion dances, and sumptuous feasts. Conversely, Rosh Hashanah, the Jewish New Year, is a solemn occasion marked by reflection and atonement and sweetened with apples and honey.

6.2. Love Across Borders

February witnesses several countries painted in crimson hues as they celebrate love- St. Valentine's Day in the West, Qixi in China, or the Week of Sweetness in Argentina. But for a unique exploration, head over to South Korea, where the 14th of every month is a "love day", like "Kiss Day" in June and "Hug Day" in December.

6.3. Spring Celebrations

As winter recedes, spring blooms with lively festivals. The Indian festival of Holi, or the Festival of Colors, celebrates spring with vibrantly tinted powders thrown to the sky. Japan's Cherry Blossom Festival, Hanami, inspires quiet contemplation amidst pastel-pink cherry blossoms, while America's Groundhog Day takes a fun spin on the changing season.

6.4. The Holy Month of Ramadan and Eid

For Muslims worldwide, Ramadan is a sacred period of fasting, introspection, and prayer, culminating in the joyous celebration of Eid-al-Fitr, marked by feasts and charitable acts.

6.5. Summer Solstice Festivities

Migrating towards mid-year, cultures globally commemorate the longest day of the year. Sweden's Midsommar Festival revolves around an enormous Maypole, with Swedes feasting, singing, and dancing into the night. Stonehenge in England witnesses a magical sunrise, while the Inti Raymi in Peru involves massive parades and rituals honoring the Sun god.

6.6. Autumns and Harvests

The calendar now turns to festivals marking harvests. In the Jewish calendar, Sukkot is a joyful eight-day thanksgiving period. Meanwhile, Chuseok, a Korean celebration, involves offering thanks to ancestors with rice cakes. From Nigeria, the New Yam Festival celebrates the yam harvest with exuberant dances and music.

6.7. Fall Festivities

And who can forget October's widespread Halloween frolics!

Alternatively, Mexico's Dia de Muertos colors fall with vibrant marigold blossoms, golden candle lights and presents to honor the dearly departed.

6.8. Winter Celebrations

Finally, the year-end brings forth a myriad of winter celebrations. From the familial warmth of American and Canadian Thanksgiving to the riotous parties of Brazil's Carnival, and from the colorful lights of Diwali, the Hindu Festival of Lights, to the joy of giving during Christmas, the world sparkles with festive joy.

This is just a glimpse of the world's calendar of festivities. The true experiences lie in immersing oneself in these rich traditions and celebrations, to share a smile, a prayer, a dance, and a meal, becoming threads in the global tapestry of cultures. Ultimately, it's not about the date on the calendar, but rather the spirit of unity, joy, and understanding these celebrations foster. Every celebration is a step further in the journey towards global camaraderie - a testament of our shared human experience. As we raise our glasses to toast the next celebration, let us also raise our understanding and appreciation of our beautifully diverse and interconnected world.

Chapter 7. Cities that Never Sleep: Exploring the World's Famous Metropolises

In the hue and cry of everyday life, there lies a hidden rhythm orchestrated by bustling cityscapes that seldom fall silent. Let's begin this sonic exploration of cities that remain awake all night and, on a global scale, offer something unique to the wandering nocturnal.

7.1. The Glittering New York

Often termed the city that never sleeps, New York exhibits a seamless blend of vibrant cultures, reflected through its music, food, arts, and nightlife. The iconic Times Square, often dubbed Crossroads of the World, buzzes with a kinetic frenzy. Countless restaurants, jazz bars, Broadway theaters, and street side delis remain aglow until well after midnight.

Across the East River, Brooklyn offers a more laid-back nighttime experience. Williamsburg's stylish speakeasies and the Smorgasburg Night Market's sumptuous food stalls mix warm community spirit with hipster vibes.

7.2. Tokyo's Neon Glow

Tokyo transforms into a riot of colors and lights post sunset. From singing your heart out in a 'karaoke-kan' to walking down the dazzling streets of Shinjuku and Shibuya, or tasting fresh sushi at 2 a.m. in the Tsukiji Fish Market, the city offers an array of nocturnal exploits.

The Robot Restaurant showcases the uniqueness of Japanese

entertainment, while the Golden Gai and Omoide Yokocho give a sense of the city's bygone Showa era. Moreover, Tokyo's vending machines, operational round-the-clock, can provide you with everything from hot meals to portable WiFi.

7.3. Enigmatic Paris

The 'City of Lights' unveils an enchanting persona after sundown. Stroll alongside the Seine with Parisian treats like crepes and "vin chaud". The illuminated Eiffel Tower and the 'nuit blanche' art festivals add a magical touch.

Imbibe French history in the Latin Quarter's literary cafés, or enjoy live music and performances at the Marais. Paris' iconic cabaret shows, like the Moulin Rouge and Crazy Horse, embody the city's sensual allure.

7.4. Mumbai – A Mosaic of Cultures

Mumbai, or Bombay as it is fondly called, thrives on its dichotomy. Serving as India's financial hub, the city's nightlife pulsates at its myriad upscale clubs and discos. Cutting through social strata, the sea-facing Marine Drive becomes the common ground for dreamers, offering solace with hot 'chai' and 'bhutta'.

Street food culture defines the city's nights. Experience Mumbai's underbelly on a late-night food tour; savor delectable kebabs at Bade Miya, or the famous street-side "pav bhaji" outside Juhu Beach. Discover vibrant markets buzzing till late, like Crawford Market and Chor Bazaar.

7.5. Electric Hong Kong

Enveloped in neon lights, Hong Kong swells with an electrifying energy after dark. With an eclectic blend of sophisticated watering holes in Lan Kwai Fong and the timeless charm of bazaars in Kowloon, the city never fails to captivate.

Taste Hong Kong's distinct cuisine at Temple Street Night Market, or visit "dai pai dongs", open-air street restaurants. Candlelit junk boat rides in Victoria Harbor and the 'Symphony of Lights' show further accentuate the city's night charm.

These metropolises symbolize humanity's vibrant make-up – continually evolving, spinning tales in their unique ways. Swathed in the sea of twinkling lights under the ink-black skies, they serve as a reminder of the dynamic lineage of cultures that pulsate through the veins of our world. Explore, embrace, and evolve in these cities that never slumber – they sure promise to offer you an experience that resonates with the rhythms of the night in perpetuity.

Chapter 8. Off the Beaten Path: Unearthing Hidden Cultural Gems

To truly experience the depth and breadth of any region, one must venture off the well-trodden tourist trails and dig deeper into the heart of local cultures. This chapter embarks on a journey through less-discovered parts of the world, exploring their untapped cultural potentials and revealing hidden treasures.

8.1. The Allure of Untouched Cultures

The beauty of travel lies not just in the exotic locations and stunning landscapes, but in the fascinating cultural insights that they offer. From the rare dialects spoken in secluded towns to the unique art forms curated over centuries in hidden villages, there is a world of cultural gems waiting to be explored. These cultural experiences not only enrich our understanding of the world but also make us more empathetic individuals.

8.2. Unveiling Hidden Cultural Gems Across Continents

This section takes you on a journey across continents into some of the lesser-known regions that are cultural hotspots in their own right. Journey into the heart of Africa to the tribes of Chad, head to the icy tundra's beauty in Greenland, or investigate the richness of cultures in the remote islands of Indonesia. These little-known places offer a treasure trove of stories, customs, and traditions, each more intriguing than the other.

8.3. Western Mongolia: An Encounter with the Nomads

In the expansive plains of Western Mongolia, the deep cultural roots of the nomadic tribes showcase humanity's enduring relationship with nature. From the Kazakh eagle hunters to the unique tradition of 'Naadam', a warrior-like competition featuring wrestling, horse racing, and archery, the cultural wealth is untapped and wholly immersive.

8.4. The Tribes of Chad: An Unconventional African Expedition

Moving towards Chad in Africa, the tribes of the Tibesti Mountains remain an undiscovered secret. Known for their cave art, innovative musical instruments, exceptional dance form, and their distinct lifestyle, these tribes offer a glimpse of Africa as you have never seen before.

8.5. Greenland: Culture Beneath the Ice

On the other end of the world teetering on the edge of the Arctic, Greenland is not just your conventional icy wonderland. Its colorful settlements, legends of myths and monsters, hauntingly beautiful throat singing, and a deep love for sled dogs paint a vibrant cultural picture against the stark white backdrop.

8.6. The Remote Archipelego, Indonesia: An Island of Many Cultures

Each island of Indonesia's remote archipelago boasts unique cultural aspects, from the intricate 'Ikat' weavings of Flores Island to the centuries-old 'Bissu' gender philosophy of Sulawesi. It is a microcosm of cultural surprises waiting to be discovered.

8.7. Tips and Pointers for Culture-centric Travel

Exploring cultural retreats necessitates a certain respect and openness towards unknown customs and traditions. From immersing oneself in the local lifestyle to learning a few phrases in the local language, these efforts can significantly enhance the cultural experience. This section lists down suggestions to make the best out of a trip to these culturally rich regions.

8.8. Culinary Delights and Traditional Cuisine

Food is an inseparable element of culture and offers a taste of a place's heritage and history. When in these regions, indulge in their local cuisines like the hearty stews in Greenland, the savory 'Airag' in Mongolia or the spicy 'Djenkoume' in Chad. The flavors will speak volumes about the regions' cultures.

8.9. Local Festivities and Celebrations

Local festivities offer an exceptional insight into a region's culture. They're a spectacle of traditions, customs, and cultural richness. Participating in such celebrations can be a joyfully immersive experience for any traveler.

8.10. Sharing Stories with Locals

Engaging with locals is one of the most effective ways to understand the fabric of a country's culture. Exchange stories, anecdotes, fables, and feel the pulse of their lifestyle, connecting on a fundamentally human level.

In this exploration of lesser-known corners of the world, one can unveil an array of diverse, vibrant cultures, each a gem in its unique way. These uncharted territories offer an opportunity to step away from the humdrum of mainstream tourist spots and plunge into an enriching cultural experience. After all, every hidden cultural gem rekindles the essence of travel – exploring the unknown and understanding the diversity of human existence. Every turn, every path taken, every culture discovered is an affirmation of the world's rich and diverse heritage waiting to be explored and cherished.

Chapter 9. Preserving the Past: Witnessing History through Heritage Sites

As we step into the realm of heritage sites, we delve into the pulsating heart of human history. These sites provide an opportunity to time travel, supporting our understanding of the past while opening a window into expansive cultures, vibrant civilizations, their stupendous achievements, upheavals, triumphs, and defeats.

9.1. The Timeless Charm of Heritage Sites

Our journey starts amidst the architectural grandeur of heritage sites. They serve as the symbols of human accomplishment, representing various periods of history. Heritage sites engage us by revealing the life and times of our ancestors, their stories etched in stone, bronze, and intricate carvings. Whether it's the awe-inspiring Egyptian Pyramids presenting an incredible glimpse into ancient Egyptian civilization or the Great Wall of China, an impressive symbol of resilience and innovation, every heritage site is a testament to human endeavor that has withstood the test of time.

Heritage sites are not just relics of the past; they continue to be living entities shaped by time, maintaining an intrinsic relationship with their environments and serving as centers for cultural expressions and practices.

9.2. Preserving the Heritage: A Global Endeavor

Safeguarding these irreplaceable assets underscores the acts of various international organizations. Prominent among them is UNESCO, the United Nations Educational, Scientific and Cultural Organization. Its World Heritage Site program catalogues, names, and conserves sites of significant cultural or natural importance. By promoting collective responsibility, UNESCO encourages respect and preservation of our shared heritage.

Check out the "World Heritage Map and List," extending over nearly 1000 sites globally. It offers a bounty of travel ideas, each one steeped in human history and cultural distinctiveness.

9.3. A Page From Our Shared History

Let's embark on a virtual tour, stopping first at Athens, home to the world-renowned Acropolis. The Parthenon, the iconic temple dedicated to Athena, the city's patron goddess, showcases Greek architecture's timeless beauty. Its pillars still echo tales of the golden age of Athens.

Next, marvel at the enigmatic Stonehenge in UK, a prehistoric monument whose origin and purpose remain subjects of active debate. Stonehenge reminds us of our longstanding quest to comprehend the universe, from arranging stones in careful astronomy-aligned patterns to modern deep-space telescopes.

In India, we encounter the Taj Mahal, a mausoleum of everlasting love and an architectural masterpiece showcasing Moghul art. Its white marble façade changes color with the day's light, mirroring the love's various shades.

9.4. The Heritage Trail: Itinerary of a Lifetime

An essential part of this cultural journey surrounds planning an itinerary that leads you through these sites, allowing you to appreciate not just the sites themselves but the context surrounding them. It includes understanding their significance within their local communities, participation in local festivals, sampling indigenous cuisine, and appreciating regional art.

Destination	Signature Heritage Site	Local Delicacy	Traditional Festival
Athens	The Acropolis	Moussaka	Apokries (Greek Carnival)
England	Stonehenge	Cornish Pasty	Summer Solstice Festival
Agra, India	Taj Mahal	Mughlai Biryani	Taj Mahotsav

Learning the history and heritage behind the sites amplifies your travel experience, rooting you in the realities of the cultures you explore, providing an unparalleled learning opportunity.

9.5. The Responsibility of Respect

While we consume the visual, intellectual, and spiritual banquet offered by heritage sites, we must remember to play our part in their preservation. It involves respecting local customs, minimizing environmental impact, and acknowledging our role as temporary stewards of these precious historical treasures.

Let's embark on this enlightening journey, witnessing history through heritage sites, basking in their stories, understanding their cultural significance, and ensuring their protection for future generations. From the towering Egyptian Pyramids to murmuring stone edifices of Stonehence, and from marbled beauty of Taj Mahal to stunning Grecian temples, every trip will be a fulfilling voyage into the rich cultural tapestry of our shared human experience.

Chapter 10. Dressed in Culture: An Exploration of Traditional Attire

From the intricate embroidery of a Chinese cheongsam to the flowing grace of an Indian sari, clothing speaks volumes about a society's history and values. Traditional attire often denotes identity, mirrors societal changes, and holds significant symbolism imbued by centuries of cultural expression. In this exploration, we journey through different regions, understanding the nuances of traditional attire, their origins, the heft of symbolism they bear, and the longevity they enjoy in contemporary fashion.

10.1. Encased in Silk and Symmetry: The Chinese Cheongsam

The Cheongsam, also known as the Qipao, epitomizes traditional Chinese attire. It is an exquisite expression of elegance and grace – a long, high-collared silk dress adorned with detailed embroideries or prints. As we go back to the Tang Dynasty (618-907 AD), we encounter the origins of this garment when women started embracing high necklines, tight waists, and slender cuts in their clothing.

Traditional Cheongsam evokes a sense of timelessness. The prints often have symbolic references, such as lotus flowers for purity or dragons for power. The Cheongsam's evolution into the modern fashion landscape is a testament to its adaptability, retaining its core elements yet continually reinventing its presence in modern wardrobes.

10.2. Fabric of Nationhood: The Indian Sari

The sari is deeply rooted in the Indian nation's fabric, spanning multiple regions, religions, and eras. Comprising of a long piece of cloth, typically 5 to 9 yards, draped around the body in various styles, the sari has been a ubiquitous part of Indian women's attire for over 5000 years.

While each region has its unique draping style, correspondingly, the sari's design also varies across diverse parts of India. You cannot miss the sheer extravagance of a vibrantly woven Kanjivaram silk from Tamil Nadu. In contrast, a simple yet elegant white sari with a red border from West Bengal exemplifies minimalistic charm.

From the traditional handloom weaves to the popular Bollywood inspired designs, the sari paradoxically represents continuity and change in Indian society. It remains a cherished garment, worn for occasions that span from the everyday to the most special.

10.3. Traversing the African Checkered Plains: The Maasai Shuka

If you traverse the African Savannah, you will undoubtedly encounter the Maasai people – a community renowned for maintaining traditional lifestyles amidst rapidly modernizing world. Their distinctive attire, a vibrant multi-colored blanket called the 'Shuka,' arises from their deep-rooted customs.

The Shuka, generally worn in shades of red, is both a fashion statement and a survival tool. The bright color alerts wild animals, and the durable cloth protects from harsh weather. The intricate plaid pattern bears a striking resemblance to the Scottish tartan, hinting at the influx of Scottish influence in the late 19th century.

Today, the Shuka's bold colors and patterns have been assimilated into global fashion trends, thanks to social media and African diasporic communities. It remains a compelling symbol of African heritage and resilience.

10.4. Whirling Garments of Anatolia: The Turkish Kaftan

No history of attire is complete without mentioning the Turkish Kaftan—a garment whose influence spread from sultanate courts to the high fashion catwalks of the 21st century. Worn by the rich and poor alike, the traditional Kaftan is a long robe with wide, flowing sleeves, crafted from a myriad of rich textiles like silk, cashmere, and cotton.

The kaftans of the Ottoman sultans, painstakingly handcrafted with gold embroidery and precious gems, symbolized their power and status. The garment evolved over the centuries, influenced by various cultural exchanges, particularly during the Ottoman empire expansion.

Contemporary iterations of the Kaftan span beach cover-ups, evening wear, and even wedding dresses – a testament to the garment's versatility and enduring appeal. The Kaftan embodies Turkey's rich history, its intersection of cultures, and its impact on global fashion trends.

Through our journey across diverse cultures and their traditional attire, we grasp not only the aesthetic appeal of these garments but also the rich cultural tapestry they originate from. As we appreciate their beauty and sophistication, let us also respect the deep cultural heritage embroiled in each stitch and fold. The next time you encounter a traditional piece of attire, remember – it's much more than just a garment; it's a story – of its people, land, and history. Let us keep buzzing the loom of cultural exploration as we continue our voyage to the next exciting destination of our journey.

Chapter 11. The Journey's End: Reflecting and Integrating Cultural Experiences

Travel is a journey of the senses - sight, sound, taste, touch, and, most crucially, the spirit. The bustling markets, the verdant landscapes, the ancient temples, the culinary delights - they all become cherished memories, embedded into your psyche, forming integral parts of your identity. As we journey across the globe, these experiences weave together to create an intricate tapestry of personal and cultural revelations. However, arriving at our journey's end signifies not a conclusion, but the beginning of a different exploration - reflecting on and integrating our cultural experiences.

11.1. The Art of Reflection

Upon arriving home, travel experiences continue to remain fresh in memory. It's essential to harness these memories while they are still rich and vivid, transforming them into nourishment for personal growth. The act of reflection is not merely a passive recollection of events, but a proactive cross-examination of experiences, encouraging deeper comprehension and insight.

Reflective journaling is a potent tool in this process. Chronicling your travel experiences, capturing the nuances of the cultures you've come across facilitates personal development and cultural understanding. Pen down thoughts about the traditional music that touched your soul, the unique flavors that excited your palate, or the stories that moved your spirit. Write about the people you met, the shared moments of laughter and camaraderie. Assimilate your senses into words, etching your experiences into the pages of your travel journals.

11.2. Embracing Cultural Integration

Experiencing diverse cultures extends beyond mere travel; it becomes an inherent part of your existence, a part of your DNA. Cultural integration is about absorbing the wisdom of ages, understanding the values and norms of different societies, and infusing aspects of their customs and practices into your lifestyle back home.

Bringing foreign elements into your daily routine can serve as a constant reminder of your enriching travel experiences. It may be as simple as incorporating a flavorful recipe from the Greek isles into your kitchen, practicing meditation techniques learned in an Indian ashram, or even adopting a Japanese KonMari method to keep your surroundings tidy.

11.3. The Tapestry of Experiences

Every culture encountered throughout your journeys adds a vibrant thread to your life's tapestry. Drawing parallels between different cultures, recognizing the shared human experiences amidst all the diversity, allows for a richer, more encompassing view of the world.

Consider creating a visual representation of your travels, a global tapestry on your wall, each piece symbolizing a culture, a memory, a lesson learned. Fusing these pieces together results in a stunning collage, mirroring your journey and the profound integrations it inspired.

11.4. Post-Journey Learning, Sharing and Inspiring

Witnessing the world leaves imprints on your heart, transforming you into a global citizen. It is valuable not only to learn from cultures but to share these learnings with your community - spreading the values of cross-cultural respect and understanding.

Initiate conversations about your experiences, orchestrate photo exhibitions, start a blog, or even hold cooking classes showcasing foreign cuisine learned abroad. The purpose of these actions is to facilitate a ripple effect - enlightening those around you and inspiring them to embark on their own journeys of cultural exploration.

11.5. The Highs and Lows: Emotional Processing

Travel is not always about cheerful discoveries and picturesque sunsets. It also encapsulates feelings of homesickness, culture shock, or witnessing harsh realities of certain societies. It's just as essential to reflect on these difficult emotions and not shelter oneself from such significant parts of the journey.

Unfiltered penning of these feelings in a journal, or sharing them with a confidant, usually aids in the emotional processing. Understanding how these lows affected you, helps in enriching your empathy and resilience skills, further shaping your personality and worldview.

11.6. The Journey within: Soulful Transformation

Finally, acknowledging the changes within you. Internal transformation is the true Journey's End, though the external journey may have culminated. Review the shifts in your perspective, the expanded horizons of your mind, the depths of empathy unearthed - monitor how you have evolved as a person through these cultural experiences.

The assimilation of all these experiences leads not just to a richer understanding of world cultures, but a profound comprehension of your own culture and identity. In this constantly spinning globe, reflecting and integrating cultural experiences fosters individual growth and bridges gaps between societies — a beautiful journey indeed, from here to there, and within.